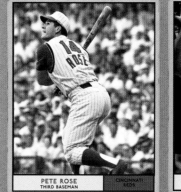

PETE ROSE
THIRD BASEMAN

CINCINNATI
REDS

JOHNNY BENCH
CATCHER

CINCINNATI
REDS

THE STORY OF THE CINCINNATI REDS

Published by Creative Education
P.O. Box 227, Mankato, Minnesota 56002
Creative Education is an imprint of The Creative Company
www.thecreativecompany.us

Design and production by Blue Design
Art direction by Rita Marshall
Printed by Corporate Graphics in the United States of America

Photographs by Corbis (Bettmann, Underwood & Underwood), Getty Images (APA, Chicago History Museum, Diamond Images, Focus on Sport, John Grieshop/MLB Photos, Heinz Kluetmeier/Sports Illustrated, Bob Levey, Andy Lyons, MLB Photos, Ronald C. Modra/Sports Imagery, National Baseball Hall of Fame/MLB Photos, Lucy Nicholson/AFP, Photo File/MLB Photos, Donavan Reese, Robert Riger, Joe Robbins, Mark Rucker/Transcendental Graphics, Joe Robbins, Paul Schutzer/Time & Life Pictures, Tony Tomsic/MLB Photos, Kevin Winter)

Library of Congress Cataloging-in-Publication Data

Goodman, Michael E.
The story of the Cincinnati Reds / by Michael E. Goodman.
p. cm. — (Baseball: the great American game)
Includes index.
Summary: The history of the Cincinnati Reds professional baseball team from its inaugural 1869 season to today, spotlighting the team's greatest players and most memorable moments.
ISBN 978-1-60818-037-0
1. Cincinnati Reds (Baseball team)—History—Juvenile literature. I. Title. II. Series.

GV875.C65G68 2011
796.357'640977178—dc22   2010024394

CPSIA: 110310 PO1381

First Edition
9 8 7 6 5 4 3 2 1

Page 3: Left fielder Adam Dunn
Page 4: Pitcher Edinson Volquez

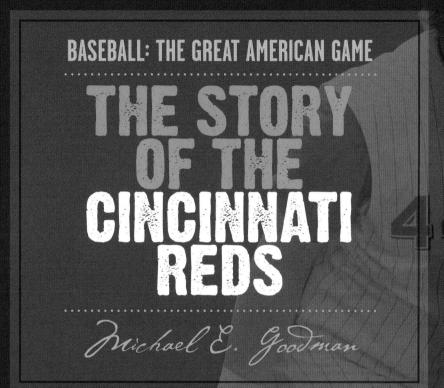

BASEBALL: THE GREAT AMERICAN GAME

THE STORY OF THE CINCINNATI REDS

Michael E. Goodman

CREATIVE EDUCATION

CONTENTS

PIONEERS IN THE MIDWEST

fter America's Revolutionary War ended in the early 1780s, many pioneers headed west across the Appalachian Mountains, looking to farm land or help build cities. One pioneering group braved the hostilities of Indian tribes to establish a settlement on the Ohio River initially called Losantiville. Hoping to attract additional settlers, town leaders soon decided the community needed a more distinctive name. That new name came from the territory's governor, General Arthur St. Clair. The governor belonged to the Society of Cincinnati, an organization of former Revolutionary War officers, so he suggested naming the town Cincinnati.

Cincinnati quickly became the busiest port city on the Ohio River, and traders and settlers arrived by the thousands. Between 1835 and 1860, Cincinnati was the fastest-growing city in America, and its grandeur earned it a lasting nickname: "Queen City of the West." Some settlers brought the new game of baseball with them from the East, and by 1869, baseball had become so popular in Cincinnati that the first all-

Although Cincinnati is also the home of the Bengals professional football team, the "Queen City" is best known for its love of baseball.

PITCHER · EPPA RIXEY

Eppa Rixey was a perfect example of how statistics don't necessarily define a great baseball player. Tall and lanky, Rixey pitched with a big, sweeping motion that confused batters but seldom overpowered them, and he averaged only around 60 strikeouts per year. During a 21-year career that lasted into his 40s, he won a lot of games but lost a lot, too. He still ranks as the "losingest" left-hander of all time, yet Cincinnati fans later voted him the best left-hander in club history. A fierce competitor on the ballfield, Rixey was remembered as a charming Virginia gentleman in everyday life.

EPPA RIXEY
PITCHER

STATS

Reds seasons: 1921–33	
Height: 6-foot-5	
Weight: 210	

- **4 seasons of 20-plus wins**
- **266–251 career record**
- **290 career complete games**
- **Baseball Hall of Fame inductee (1963)**

professional team in America was established there. The players' bright red socks gave the club its name: the Red Stockings, later shortened to simply "Reds."

Brothers Harry and George Wright helped to organize the Red Stockings. The sons of an English cricket star, they had played baseball in New York before moving west. Harry was an outfielder and pitcher. He also managed the team and was responsible for convincing players from the East to come to Cincinnati, which he did by offering tempting salaries of up to $800 a year.

George, meanwhile, was the team's shortstop and best all-around player. During the club's first season, George batted .629, slugged 49 home runs, and scored 339 runs in just 57 games! The Red Stockings won all 57 contests. Then they kept winning in 1870, extending their streak to a staggering 81 consecutive victories before losing an 11-inning thriller in New York to the Brooklyn Atlantics. The Red Stockings were not only good, they were tough. Years after his playing days were over, George Wright attended a baseball game. He came away from the contest sneering, "Imagine, players wearing gloves. We didn't need them in our day."

HARRY WRIGHT

Harry Wright is credited with pioneering many baseball standards, from the positioning of players on the field to the routine of batting practice.

In 1876, a new baseball organization, the National League (NL), was formed, and the Red Stockings became charter members. The Wrights had moved to Boston by then (where they helped form a franchise called the Braves), and the Red Stockings didn't fare too well in the new league. The club had one legitimate star, iron-armed pitcher Will "Whoop-La" White, who pitched in 76 of the team's 81 games in 1879 and won 43 of them—still a club record.

In the 1890s, the team settled near the middle of the NL standings despite the hitting exploits of center fielder James "Bug" Holliday, who twice led the NL in homers (with 19 and 13) and consistently batted over .300. By the early 1900s, the team name had been shortened to Reds, but the club's position in the standings remained the same. In fact, the Reds never finished above fifth place in the NL between 1905 and 1916.

The team's fortunes finally began to turn in 1916, when center fielder Edd Roush, a future Hall-of-Famer, arrived via a trade with the New York Giants. Roush was an outstanding hitter, twice winning NL batting titles, but he may have been an even better fielder. In 1919, everything

Playing against overmatched opponents, Cincinnati's original 1869 squad was simply unstoppable, finishing its schedule a perfect 57–0.

OPENING DAY TRADITION

Opening day of the baseball season is important in most major-league cities, but it is a true celebration in Cincinnati. From 1876 until 1989, the Cincinnati Reds were awarded the privilege of having the first game of the season take place in their home stadium. This was to honor the fact that the Cincinnati Red Stockings had been America's first officially recognized professional baseball team. Only twice during those years (in 1877 and 1966) did the Reds open the season on the road because of heavy rains at home. The tradition was finally broken in 1990, and in recent years, the first game has been scheduled in different cities—some as far away as Tokyo, Japan. Opening day festivities in Cincinnati usually included a giant parade complete with elephants, floats, and marching bands. Teachers used to allow students who presented an opening day ticket to leave school early to get to the parade and the game. Very little business was accomplished in the afternoon in Cincinnati once the game began, and many companies were closed. As one local attorney remarked, "If you're hoping to catch anyone in the office at three o'clock on opening day, good luck."

CATCHER • JOHNNY BENCH

Reds manager Sparky Anderson was once asked how Johnny Bench ranked with other catchers he had seen. "I don't want to embarrass any other catcher by comparing him to Johnny Bench," Anderson said. Bench was a rock wall when guarding home plate and had a cannon for an arm. His hands were so big that he could hold seven baseballs at a time in either one. Bench was also one of the best power-hitting catchers of all time. He is the only backstop since 1900 to have led the NL in home runs and the only catcher ever to have led the league in runs batted in (RBI) three times.

JOHNNY BENCH
CATCHER

CINCINNATI
REDS

STATS

Reds seasons: 1967–83

Height: 6-foot-1

Weight: 208

- 1,376 career RBI

- 2-time NL MVP

- 14-time All-Star

- Baseball Hall of Fame inductee (1989)

FIRST BASEMAN · TONY PEREZ

Most members of the famed "Big Red Machine" had great talent and large egos. Tony Perez was the quiet one of the group and the oil that kept the machine running smoothly. Affectionately called "Big Doggie" by his teammates, Perez knew when to crack a joke to break the tension and how to calm teammates who were feeling the pressure. He could also be counted on to supply at least 18 homers and 90 RBI every season. "[Pete] Rose, [Johnny] Bench, and I got the publicity," said second baseman Joe Morgan, "but Tony was our rock."

TONY PEREZ
FIRST BASEMAN

CINCINNATI
REDS

STATS

Reds seasons: 1964–76, 1984–86

Height: 6-foot-2

Weight: 205

• 379 career HR

• 1,652 career RBI

• 7-time All-Star

• Baseball Hall of Fame inductee (2000)

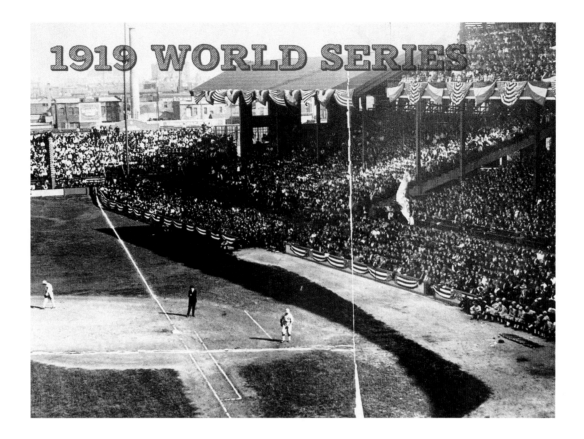

1919 WORLD SERIES

came together for Roush and his teammates. Pitchers Slim Sallee, Hod Eller, and Dutch Ruether combined for 59 wins, and the Reds captured their first NL pennant. Facing off against the American League (AL) champion Chicago White Sox in the World Series, the Reds surprised most experts by winning the series five games to three, but the final results were tainted. A great scandal arose when it was discovered that several of the White Sox players had taken bribes from gamblers to throw games, or lose on purpose. The 1919 Reds were world champions, but few people outside of Cincinnati gave them much credit for their victory.

LIGHTING UP THE LEAGUE

he Reds remained strong throughout the 1920s, coming close to winning a second NL pennant but never quite reaching the top. Led by Roush, fellow outfielder Curt Walker, and pitcher Eppa Rixey, the Reds challenged the New York Giants and the St. Louis Cardinals for league supremacy throughout the decade.

The Great Depression years of the 1930s were especially depressing for Cincinnati baseball fans. The club finished in the NL cellar every season from 1931 to 1934, and fans stopped showing up at Redland Field. Then, broadcasting executive Powell Crosley purchased the team and began making changes. Crosley persuaded Major League Baseball executives to allow the Reds to play seven night games at Cincinnati's Crosley Field during the 1935 season as a way to boost attendance. Until that time, baseball had been played strictly during the day. The experiment worked, as the Reds averaged 18,000 fans for the night contests, compared with 4,600 for day games. Soon, other major-league teams would install lights in their stadiums and begin scheduling night games.

ERNIE LOMBARDI

Ernie Lombardi (right) was often ribbed for his slowness; an opposing manager once remarked that the catcher ran "like he was carrying a piano–and the fellow tuning it." Still, Lombardi's steady bat and strong arm made him a star in the 1930s.

SECOND BASEMAN · JOE MORGAN

Most players Joe Morgan's size would bat at the very top or bottom of the lineup. Morgan batted third for the Big Red Machine teams of the 1970s—the spot reserved for a club's most consistent run producer. Between 1972 and 1977, Morgan averaged 22 home runs, 84 RBI, 118 walks, 113 runs scored, and 60 stolen bases a year. He also won five Gold Gloves for his defense. "I was one of the guys who did all they could to win," he said proudly. Today, Morgan is a television announcer who explains the intricacies of the game to viewers.

JOE MORGAN
SECOND BASEMAN

CINCINNATI
REDS

STATS

Reds seasons: 1972–79

Height: 5-foot-7

Weight: 160

- **1,133 career RBI**

- **2-time NL MVP**

- **1,865 career walks**

- **Baseball Hall of Fame inductee (1990)**

In the late 1930s, several new stars appeared under the lights in Cincinnati. Pitcher Johnny Vander Meer thrilled Reds fans when he pitched back-to-back no-hitters in June 1938. Vander Meer's battery mate, All-Star catcher Ernie Lombardi, led the team in batting. He was named the NL's Most Valuable Player (MVP) in 1938 and would eventually be enshrined in the Hall of Fame.

Lombardi was one of the slowest runners in the history of baseball, yet he still managed to win two NL batting crowns and finished with a career .306 batting average. The lumbering catcher could never beat out an infield hit and sometimes had trouble getting to first base on hard shots to the outfield. "Ernie has to hit .400 just to end up with .300," joked Reds manager Bill McKechnie.

In 1939, Lombardi, ace pitcher Bucky Walters, and hard-hitting first baseman Frank McCormick led the Reds to their first pennant in 20 years. Unfortunately, Cincinnati was swept out of the 1939 World Series by the New York Yankees. The Reds were better prepared in 1940, when they repeated as NL champs and then out-battled the Detroit Tigers in seven games for their second world championship—and this one wasn't tainted at all.

REDS

GIVING THE 1919 REDS THEIR DUE

The Reds team that captured the World Series in 1919 has never been given the respect it deserves. Most people seem to feel that the Reds would never have won that series if several Chicago White Sox players had not agreed to take bribes to throw games. But the 1919 Reds were a powerful club in their own right and may not have needed help to win. They ranked second in the NL in hitting and pitching, and they featured the NL batting champ (Edd Roush) and 3 pitchers (Slim Sallee, Hod Eller, and Dutch Ruether) who each won at least 19 games. These three hurlers accounted for all five of the Reds' victories in the series. There is also some question about whether all of the Chicago players who were in on the fix really tried to play poorly throughout the series. Some baseball historians believe that the series was played on the level after Game 1, when expected payments from gamblers were not made to the "Black Sox." Roush had his own opinion about the Reds' victory. "One thing that has always been overlooked in this whole mess," he said, "is that we could have beaten them no matter what the circumstances. The 1919 Reds were better."

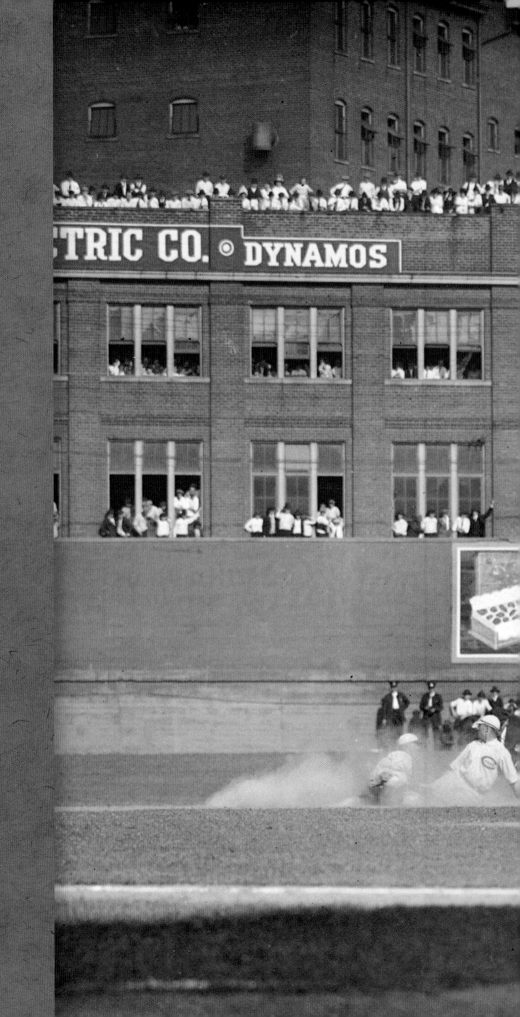

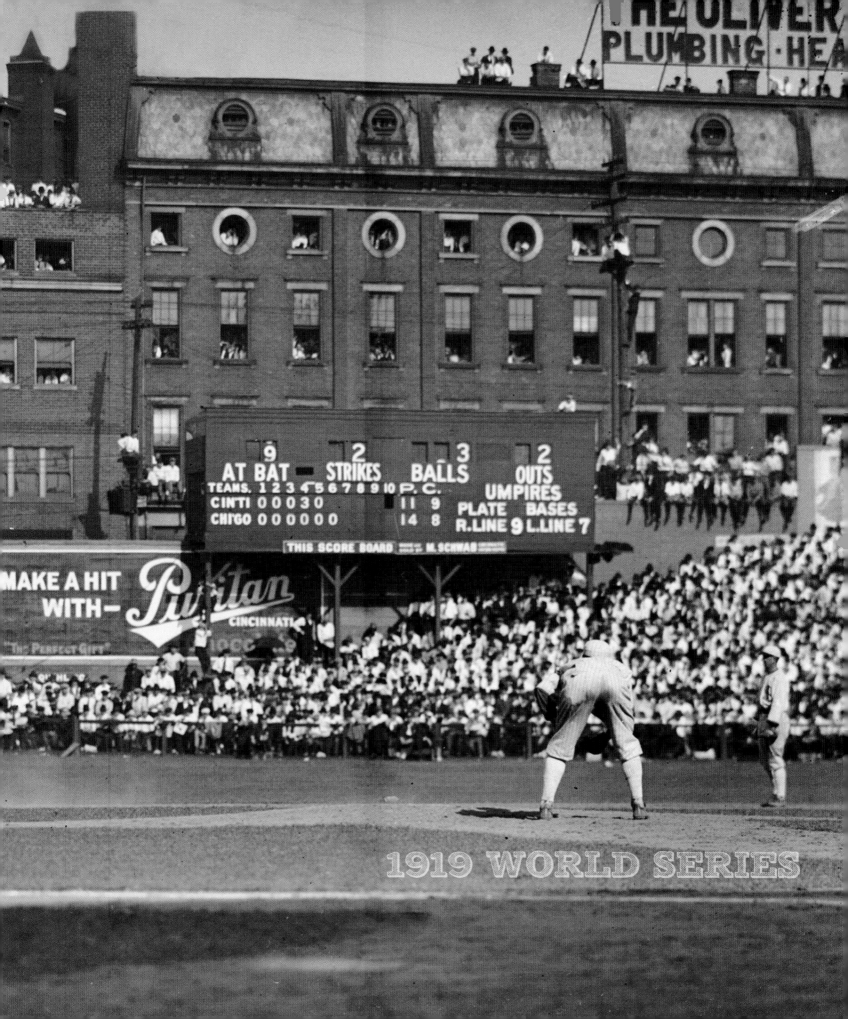

Known to fans as "Big Klu," Ted Kluszewski found his groove in 1953; over the next 4 seasons, he slugged 171 home runs.

Cincinnati's pitching remained strong into the 1940s, but the club's hitting and scoring declined. As a result, the Reds slipped to the bottom half of the league for a decade. Then, in the mid-1950s, manager Birdie Tebbetts built an offensive powerhouse that featured muscleman first baseman Ted Kluszewski and slugging outfielders Wally Post and Gus Bell. In 1956, that nucleus expanded to include a 20-year-old rookie outfielder named Frank Robinson, whose impressive skills at the plate and in the field swiftly raised him to superstar status.

Robinson crowded the plate and dared pitchers to try to put the ball past him. Many times he had to hit the dirt to avoid an inside fastball. Then he would get up quickly and send the next pitch screaming into the outfield or stands. In the field, Robinson was just as fearless and exciting. During the first few months of his rookie season, the intrepid Robinson crashed into a wall and was stunned or knocked out completely six times. Each time, he got up with the help

THIRD BASEMAN · PETE ROSE

Pete Rose appeared in more major-league games than any other player, and no one played each game harder than he did. His father, a semiprofessional football player, instilled the value of sports into his son—he even kept Pete out of summer school one year so he wouldn't miss a baseball season. "People say I don't have great tools," Rose once remarked. "I make up for it by putting out a little bit more. That's my theory, to go through life hustling." Sadly, Rose could not control his competitive drive to gamble, a weakness that has kept him from entering the Hall of Fame.

PETE ROSE
THIRD BASEMAN

CINCINNATI REDS

STATS

Reds seasons: 1963–78, 1984–86

Height: 5-foot-11

Weight: 200

- **3-time NL batting champion**

- **4,256 career hits (most all-time)**

- **17-time All-Star**

- **1973 NL MVP**

DOUBLE "NO-NO"

Reds pitcher Johnny Vander Meer holds one baseball record that may never be broken. In June 1938, he pitched two consecutive no-hit, no-run games. (Breaking the record would require a pitcher to throw three "no-no's" in a row, a feat considered to be virtually impossible.) Vander Meer was in his first full major-league season in 1938. The young lefty was a hard thrower, but he also had a tendency to be wild. On June 11 at Cincinnati's Crosley Field, he walked three batters and struck out four in a 3–0 no-hitter against the Boston Braves. Four days later, Vander Meer took on the Dodgers in the first night game ever held at Brooklyn's Ebbets Field. This time, he issued eight walks and needed spectacular fielding from his teammates to preserve the 6–0 no-hitter. Vander Meer almost self-destructed in the ninth inning. He walked three Dodgers batters to load the bases before getting shortstop Leo Durocher to pop up for the final out. While no major-league pitcher has ever equaled Vander Meer's performance, the one who came closest was Reds hurler Ewell "The Whip" Blackwell. In 1944, Blackwell came within two outs of a second straight no-hitter before having to settle for a one-hit shutout.

of his manager or teammates and kept on playing. Finally, Tebbetts told him, "Look, Frank, the next time you hit a wall, I'm not going to leave the dugout. I'm getting too old to walk 450 feet for nothing."

Led by Robinson, the Reds finally returned to the top of the NL in 1961. "Robby" batted .323 with 37 homers that season and was named league MVP. Center fielder Vada Pinson helped spark the offense with a .343 average, while pitchers Joey Jay and Jim O'Toole combined for 40 of the team's 93 wins. Playing on the grand stage of the World Series for the first time in 21 years, Cincy could not handle the AL champion Yankees, though, whose lineup featured slugging stars Roger Maris and Mickey Mantle. The Yanks dominated the Reds, but revenge was coming.

BUILDING THE "MACHINE"

obinson played four more solid seasons with the Reds before being traded to the Baltimore Orioles following the 1965 campaign. A new group of stars had begun arriving in Cincinnati, however, and they would form one of the most dominant teams in baseball history—the "Big Red Machine."

The first cog of the machine was a hometown boy named Pete Rose. Rose was strong, tough, and versatile. During his days with the Reds, he was an All-Star first baseman, second baseman, third baseman, and outfielder. A great student of baseball history, Rose played with the intensity of old-time great Ty Cobb, whose career hitting records Rose would eventually break. Rose's aggressive play earned him the nickname "Charlie Hustle." He slid hard into bases and even sprinted down the first-base line when he drew a walk. "If you play an aggressive, hustling game, it forces your opponents into errors," he explained. Rose's competitive nature would drive him to the top of baseball's record books in career games played, at bats, and total hits.

Although he was not exceptionally fast,
Pete Rose was an outstanding base runner,
combining rare aggression with great instincts.

SHORTSTOP · BARRY LARKIN

When he was only five years old and growing up in Cincinnati, Barry Larkin told friends that he would someday replace his idol, Dave Concepción, as the Reds' shortstop. He was true to his word. When Larkin joined the Reds in 1986 at age 22, Concepción moved over to second base to make room for the youngster. During 19 seasons with the Reds, Larkin's leadership was just as important as his skill on the field. Teammates credit a team meeting Larkin called late in the 1990 season with keeping the club driving toward an NL pennant and an eventual World Series title.

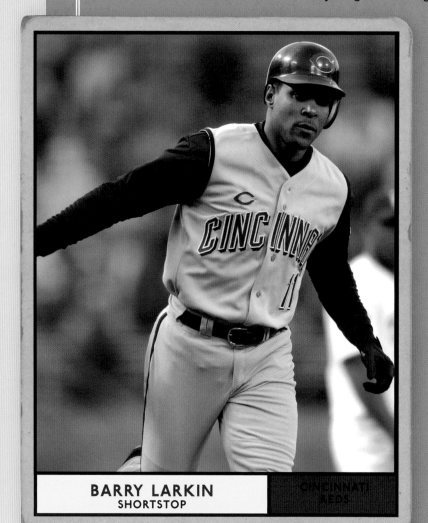

BARRY LARKIN
SHORTSTOP

CINCINNATI
REDS

STATS

Reds seasons: 1986–2004

Height: 6 feet

Weight: 185

- **5,858 career assists**

- **2,340 career hits**

- **12-time All-Star**

- **1995 NL MVP**

Rose specialized in getting on base so he could be driven in by All-Star teammates such as catcher Johnny Bench and first baseman Tony Perez. Bench, who hailed from tiny Binger, Oklahoma, was to become the finest defensive catcher in NL history as well as a superb power hitter. Perez, a native of Cuba, was noted for his consistency. He drove in 90 or more runs in 10 straight seasons in Cincinnati and was a solid contributor in the field as well. While Rose, Bench, and Perez spearheaded the Reds' offense, the club's top pitcher in the 1960s was Jim Maloney. The right-hander fired two no-hitters during his career and still ranks as the Reds' all-time strikeout leader.

When the Reds left Crosley Field for the brand-new Riverfront Stadium in 1970, a dynasty was emerging. The 1970 club, managed by Sparky Anderson, won a team-record 102 games to capture the NL pennant but fell quietly to Frank Robinson's Orioles in the World Series.

The final component of the Machine was added in 1972, when the Reds acquired second baseman Joe Morgan from the Houston Astros. At 5-foot-7 and 160 pounds, Morgan didn't look imposing. But he was quick and powerful and soon proved that he was one of the most

LEFT FIELDER · GEORGE FOSTER

Quiet by nature, George Foster was one of the least colorful members of the Big Red Machine. He let his powerful bat do all the talking. Foster began his Reds career riding the bench, but he pounded the ball every opportunity he was given and convinced manager Sparky Anderson to make him a regular in the lineup. Few hitters have had a more dominant season than Foster did in 1977: he batted .320, with 52 home runs and 149 RBI, on his way to being named NL MVP. Foster also tied an NL record by leading the league in RBI for three consecutive years.

GEORGE FOSTER
LEFT FIELDER

CINCINNATI
REDS

STATS

Reds seasons: 1971–81

Height: 6-foot-1

Weight: 185

- 348 career HR

- 1,239 career RBI

- 5-time All-Star

- 2-time NL leader in HR and RBI

BEST SERIES EVER?

The 1975 World Series between the Reds and Boston Red Sox was a classic. The Big Red Machine had romped to the NL pennant that year, winning a club-record 108 games—20 more than the second-place Los Angeles Dodgers. The Reds were favored to defeat the Red Sox, but Boston got off to a quick start, winning 6–0 in Game 1 behind pitching ace Luis Tiant. Cincy won three of the next four contests, thanks largely to great relief pitching by Rawly Eastwick, and was leading Game 6 by a score of 6–3 going into the bottom of the eighth inning in Boston. Then a dramatic three-run homer by Bernie Carbo, a former Reds outfielder, sent the contest into extra innings. In the bottom of the 12th, Red Sox catcher Carlton Fisk slugged a now-famous home run shot that banked off the foul pole in left field to give Boston the win and force a seventh game. The Red Sox jumped out to a 3–0 lead in Game 7, but the Reds stormed back, with Joe Morgan's bloop single in the ninth inning bringing home the winning run. The triumph gave the Reds their first championship in 35 years.

JOE MORGAN

complete players in the game. Morgan slashed singles and doubles, stole bases, hit home runs, and made spectacular plays in the field.

The Reds became the dominant team of the NL Western Division throughout the 1970s. (The two major leagues had each been split into two divisions in 1969.) Cincinnati won 12 total championships during the decade—6 NL West titles, 4 NL pennants, and back-to-back world championships in 1975 and 1976. The two World Series victories were a contrast in style. The 1975 series against the Boston Red Sox is considered one of the most exciting and well-matched series of all time, going down to the last inning of Game 7 before a Morgan single propelled Cincy to the title. The 1976 series, on the other hand, was a complete massacre, as the Reds crushed the Yankees in four straight games. "What a ballclub that was," Sparky Anderson recalled years later. "Morgan, Doggie [Perez], Bench, Rose, along with [right fielder] Ken Griffey, [left fielder] George Foster, and [shortstop] Davey Concepción. Those guys were the best I've ever seen. They spoiled me rotten as a manager."

o 1976, Joe Morgan was the
ut" in the league, leading NL hitters
ercentage all three seasons.

A RIVERFRONT RESURGENCE

 y 1980, the Big Red Machine had started to sputter, and soon the club slipped toward the bottom of the NL West. In an effort to turn things around, club management made a trade with the Montreal Expos in August 1984 to bring back Pete Rose (who had left in 1978) as player/manager. Rose piloted the team back above .500 in 1985 and made baseball history that September when he smacked a sharp single into left-center at Riverfront Stadium for his record-breaking 4,192nd hit. The following year, Rose retired as a player to concentrate on managing.

Among the talented stars who played for Rose in the late 1980s were shortstop Barry Larkin, third baseman Chris Sabo, and outfielder Eric Davis. Larkin, a double-threat at the plate and in the field, anchored the Reds' infield from 1986 to 2004 and ranks in the top three in club history in steals, hits, and runs scored. Sabo endeared himself to Reds fans with his constant hustle, and Davis was the team's main power and base-stealing

CENTER FIELDER · EDD ROUSH

Edd Roush was known for his amazingly strong hands. Although he weighed only 170 pounds, Roush used bats that weighed 46 to 48 ounces—among the heaviest in the game. Roush wielded these short, round bats to spray hits all over the field or to lay down perfect bunts. He was one of the most feared and consistent hitters during his era, batting over .300 in 11 straight seasons. Roush was also a terrific defensive center fielder who seemed to know how to position himself perfectly for every opposing batter who came to the plate.

EDD ROUSH
CENTER FIELDER

STATS

Reds seasons: 1916–26, 1931

Height: 5-foot-11

Weight: 170

- .323 career BA

- only 260 career strikeouts (in 7,363 at bats)

- 2-time NL batting champion

- Baseball Hall of Fame inductee (1962)

threat as well as a spectacular—and sometimes reckless—fielder. "I'm supposed to steal bases. I'm supposed to hit home runs, too," said Davis. "I've run into walls. I've jumped over walls to make catches." That style thrilled fans but often resulted in injuries that kept him out of the lineup.

The Reds had finally begun to move up in the NL West standings when Cincy fans were dealt a crushing blow in August 1989: Rose was accused of betting on games, including those involving his own team, and was banished from baseball for life by Commissioner Bartlett Giamatti. Rose would proclaim his innocence for many years before finally admitting his wrongdoing in 2004. The ban continues to be upheld, and Rose has consequently been denied induction into the Baseball Hall of Fame.

Fortunately, just when local fans needed a lift, the Reds gave it to them. Under new manager Lou Piniella, the 1990 club won its first nine games and never let up, topping the NL West at 91–71. The core of that team was a trio of nearly unhittable relief pitchers—Randy Meyers, Norm Charlton, and Rob Dibble—who were known collectively as the "Nasty Boys." Piniella used one or more of the trio in nearly every game during the season, and they usually dominated opposing batters.

ROB DIBBLE   NORM CHARLTON

The Reds kept winning in the postseason, defeating the Pittsburgh Pirates in six games in the NL Championship Series (NLCS) before sweeping the defending champion Oakland A's in the World Series in one of the most stunning upsets in the history of the "Fall Classic." Summing up the Reds' improbable victory, first baseman Todd Benzinger said, "The A's have the best talent in baseball, but we have the best team."

The Reds were champs again, but the excitement in Cincinnati was short-lived, as injuries to key players made it difficult for the

KEN SR.

KEN JR.

ALL IN THE FAMILY

When Ken Griffey Jr. joined the Reds in 2000, he became an official member of the team. But he had been a part of the Reds family for most of his life, as his father, outfielder Ken Griffey Sr., was a valuable player in Cincinnati for 12 seasons between 1973 and 1990. The Griffeys are just one of many father-son duos with connections to the Reds. Sons of two other members of the Big Red Machine—Pete Rose and Tony Perez—later played for short periods of time in Cincinnati. Infielder Pete Rose Jr. is the only Reds player who has been allowed to wear uniform number 14 since his father was forced to retire in 1989, and first baseman Eduardo Perez played parts of three seasons in Cincinnati in the 1990s. Brothers Bret and Aaron Boone played together in the infield for the Reds in the 1990s, and their father Bob was Cincinnati's manager from 2001 to 2003. Three generations of the Bell family have also played for the Reds: outfielder Gus (1950s) and third basemen Buddy (1980s) and Mike (2000).

RIGHT FIELDER · FRANK ROBINSON

Frank Robinson played hard and angry. He would stand close to the plate in a deep crouch and glare over his left shoulder toward the pitcher, daring him to pitch inside. "Pitchers did me a favor when they knocked me down," Robinson said. "It made me more determined. I wouldn't let that pitcher get me out." "Robby" achieved several big-league firsts during his career: first player to win an MVP award in both leagues, first player to hit 200 homers in each league, and first African American manager when he took over the helm of the Cleveland Indians in 1975.

FRANK ROBINSON
RIGHT FIELDER

CINCINNATI REDS

STATS

Reds seasons: 1956–65

Height: 6-foot-1

Weight: 195

- 586 career HR

- 1966 AL Triple Crown winner (leader in BA, HR, and RBI)

- 12-time All-Star

- Baseball Hall of Fame inductee (1982)

MANAGER · BILL McKECHNIE

As an infielder for the Pirates, Braves, and Yankees, Bill McKechnie was an average player at best. But he studied the game carefully and made his mark as a manager. Before taking over in Cincinnati in 1938, McKechnie had already won NL pennants in both Pittsburgh (1925) and St. Louis (1928). When his Reds teams captured league titles in both 1939 and 1940, he became the only manager ever to take three different franchises to the World Series. A religious man nicknamed "Deacon Bill," McKechnie was known for his likeable personality and patience.

BILL McKECHNIE
MANAGER

CINCINNATI
REDS

STATS

Reds seasons as manager: 1938–46

Managerial record: 1,896–1,723

World Series championship: 1940

Baseball Hall of Fame inductee (1962)

team to win consistently in the early 1990s. Cincinnati returned to the playoffs in 1995, as Larkin was named league MVP, but it was eliminated in the NLCS by the Atlanta Braves. Unfortunately, that was the last time the team would see postseason play for the better part of two decades.

In 2000, the Reds made a major move by acquiring All-Star center fielder Ken Griffey Jr.—one of the game's top sluggers and defensive outfielders. Griffey had roots in Cincinnati; his father had been a key member of the Big Red Machine, and "Junior" had spent a lot of time as a kid at Riverfront Stadium. When he arrived for a preseason press conference before the Cincinnati media, Griffey remarked, "Well, at last I'm home."

Griffey was only 30 years old when he joined the Reds, but he had already hit 398 home runs. Reds fans had high expectations when Griffey slugged 40 homers and drove in 118 runs in 2000 to help Cincy finish second in the division. Unfortunately, Junior spent much of the next four seasons out with injuries. Talkative first baseman Sean Casey and muscular outfielder Adam Dunn tried to fill the power gap, but the club became mired below the .500 mark.

NEW STADIUM, NEW ATTITUDE

he Reds moved into a new stadium, Great American Ball Park, before the 2003 campaign. With its exciting mosaics of great Reds teams from 1869 to the era of the Big Red Machine and beyond, the new home celebrated the team's past as well as its present. Unfortunately, the new digs didn't improve the club's luck. The Reds got off to a quick start in 2004, and the season reached a high point on Father's Day, when Griffey slugged his 500th home run as his father watched from the stands. However, a few weeks later, Junior underwent season-ending hamstring surgery, and the Reds quickly fell out of the pennant race. Still, fans enjoyed watching Dunn slug 46 home runs. In 2005, he hit one that was literally an interstate blast. The majestic shot sailed so far out of Great American Ball Park that it cleared the Ohio border and landed on a piece of driftwood on the Kentucky side of the Ohio River.

The Reds posted two more losing seasons in 2005 and 2006 but were

GEORGE CLOONEY

A BASEBALL DREAM

In 2008, Hollywood star George Clooney was offered a contract to play baseball for a minor-league team in Dayton, Ohio. Clooney thought about the offer for a few days but ultimately turned it down. If the offer had come from the Cincinnati Reds instead, Clooney might have jumped at the chance. Ever since he was a kid growing up in the suburbs of Cincinnati and rooting for the Big Red Machine in the 1970s, Clooney had dreamed of playing major league baseball for his hometown team. A star player in high school, Clooney was even invited to try out for the Reds in 1977, when he was just 16. Unfortunately, he failed to impress Cincinnati scouts and wasn't offered a spot on the Big Red Machine or in the Reds' minor-league system. Disappointed, Clooney decided to head to Northern Kentucky University, where he chose acting over baseball. Soon he earned a few bit parts in movies and then attained stardom in the television series *ER* and several blockbuster movies. As of 2010, Clooney had yet to portray a baseball player in the movies, but he continued to cheer for the Reds and perhaps to dream of leading them to another pennant.

REDS

in the hunt for the NL Wild Card berth in 2006 until the final weeks of the season. Griffey and Dunn continued to pound the ball, hurlers Aaron Harang and Bronson Arroyo led an up-and-coming pitching rotation, and young third baseman Edwin Encarnación and second baseman Brandon Phillips offered hope for an improved infield defense. "You can't always depend on the three-run homer," said Reds general manager Wayne Krivsky as the team prepared for 2007. "We have to execute better than we did last year, doing the little things."

When the Reds continued to struggle, management brought in veteran manager Dusty Baker to oversee a new youth movement. Griffey and Dunn were both traded away in 2008, and emerging stars such as outfielder Jay Bruce, first baseman Joey Votto, and pitchers Homer Bailey and Edinson Volquez arrived. Under Baker's leadership, Votto, Bruce, and Volquez all had solid seasons in 2008 and finished in the top five in voting for NL Rookie of the Year.

As the 2009 season began, some sportswriters predicted that the Reds could challenge the St. Louis Cardinals and Chicago Cubs for the NL Central Division crown. Cincinnati posted a losing record that year, but in 2010, the Reds lived up to

Although he often struggled in the field, Edwin Encarnación gave the Reds some pop at the plate, jacking 26 homers during the 2008 season.

JOEY VOTTO

their potential, going 91–71 to win the division and make the playoffs for the first time in 15 years. Unfortunately, the hot bats of Votto, Bruce, and center fielder Drew Stubbs cooled off in the playoffs against the Philadelphia Phillies, and the usually sure-gloved Reds committed numerous fielding errors as they suffered a three-game sweep.

Since 1869, the Cincinnati Reds have been making baseball history. Thirty-three Hall-of-Famers have played all or parts of their careers in a Reds uniform, and hundreds of other stars have thrilled Queen City fans over the years. Now settled into a classy new home and led by a new generation of summer heroes, the Reds are making their fans believe that another powerhouse may soon arise on the banks of the Ohio River.

The seasoned leadership of Dusty Baker (above) and MVP award-winning efforts of Joey Votto (opposite) made Cincinnati's 2010 season one to remember.

REDS

INDEX